Noodle Recipe Book

Delicious Noodle Recipes for The Amateur Chef!

BY: Valeria Ray

License Notes

Copyright © 2019 Valeria Ray All Rights Reserved

All rights to the content of this book are reserved by the Author without exception unless permission is given stating otherwise.

The Author have no claims as to the authenticity of the content and the Reader bears all responsibility and risk when following the content. The Author is not liable for any reparations, damages, accidents, injuries or other incidents occurring from the Reader following all or part of this publication.

Table of Contents

Introduction 6

1. Asian Shrimp and Noodle Soup... 7

2. Noodles with Pork and Pickles 10

3. Lentil Noodle Soup 13

4. Brown Sauce Noodles 16

5. Egg Flower Noodle Soup... 19

6. Chiu Chow Dessert Noodles 23

7. Beef and Water Spinach Noodles 25

8. Chicken Noodle Soup.. 28

9. Long–Life Noodles 31

10. Roast Pork Noodle Soup 34

11. Two–Sides–Brown Noodles with Shredded Duck 37

12. Buddhist Vegetable Noodles 40

13. Noodles with Shredded Lamb 43

14. Hokkien Noodles with Prawns 46

15. Bang Bang Chicken Noodles.................................... 49

16. Chicken Noodle Salad 53

17. Thai Shrimp Noodle Soup....................................... 57

18. Cranberry Nectarine Salad 60

19. Vegetable Primavera 63

20. Eight Treasure Noodles... 66

21. San Choy Bau with Cellophane Noodles 69

22. Suckling Pig, Jellyfish and Noodle Salad 72

23. Spring Rain Tempura... 75

24. Chilled Somen 79

25. Curry Udon... 82

26. Moon-Viewing Noodles... 85

27. Penang Laksa... 88

28. Singapore Beehoon.. 91

29. Chilli Prawn Noodles... 94

30. Khanom Jeen With Spicy Pork 97

Conclusion 100

About the Author 101

Author's Afterthoughts 103

Introduction

Noodles are a centuries old technique and are part of several cuisines. Sweet and spicy, or thick and creamy, there are a variety of different noodle recipes that are easy to bring together and can elevate your meal to another level!

So go ahead, bring alive the flavors of these delicious noodle recipes: earthy, rich, hot and sour, softly sweet or aromatic. Infused with fresh, leafy herbs and fragrant spices, your noodle choices are now endless!

1. Asian Shrimp and Noodle Soup

This noodle soup is both easy to make and delicious at the same time!

Preparation Time: 15 minutes

Cooking Time: 15 minutes

Servings: 2

Ingredients:

- 9 cups water
- 3 ramen noodle packets
- 10 oz. frozen, cooked, peeled and deveined medium shrimp
- 2 tsp dark oriental sesame oil
- ½ tsp crushed red pepper.
- 1 cup chopped scallions
- ½ cup grated carrots

Instructions:

Take a clean and dry pot and add the water to it. Bring this up to a boil.

Now break the blocks of noodles into 4 pieces each and add them to the pot.

Cook for around 5 minutes while constantly stirring. This will ensure that the strands separate from each other. Cook until the noodles are tender.

Take the pot off the heat now. Add the shrimp and the packets of seasoning to the pot immediately. Also add the oil and the crushed peppers.

Let cool for around 2 minutes. Sprinkle the scallions and carrots over the top. You may grate some cheese over the top if you want to.

Serve hot with lime wedges.

2. Noodles with Pork and Pickles

Pickled mustard cabbage is often sold with its pickling liquid in large plastic bags. Combine with a little pork and a lot of noodles, and a state of bliss will follow presently.

Time: 45m

Serves: 4

Ingredients:

- 3 tbsp peanut oil
- 2 tbsp soy sauce
- 2 tsp sugar
- 2 tsp cornstarch
- ½ tsp salt
- 14 oz pork loin, cut into thin slices
- 1 lb. Hokkien noodles
- 1 tsp sesame oil
- 4 oz pickled mustard cabbage
- 7 oz bamboo shoots, cut into thin matchsticks
- 3 tbsp chicken stock

Instructions:

Combine 1 tablespoon peanut oil, soy sauce, sugar, cornstarch and salt in a bowl and stir pork through. Set aside for 30 minutes.

Pour boiling water over noodles in a heatproof bowl and let stand for 30 seconds. Quickly drain and rinse in cold water. Drain again, mix with sesame oil and set aside.

Rinse pickled cabbage in cold water. Dry well with paper towels and shred finely.

Heat 1 tablespoon peanut oil in a hot wok and stir fry bamboo shoots for 30 seconds. Add pickled cabbage and cook for another 30 seconds. Transfer vegetables to a bowl. Heat remaining 1 tablespoon oil and stir fry pork for about 3 minutes until well-coloured. Add stock, bamboo shoots and pickled vegetables and stir fry for 1 or 2 minutes.

Add noodles and toss well to heat through for 1 minute, then serve on a large warmed serving platter or in small Chinese bowls.

3. Lentil Noodle Soup

This hearty and delicious soup is perfect for the colder months.

Makes: 2-3 servings

Prep: 5 mins

Cook: 35 mins

Ingredients:

- 2 teaspoons extra-virgin olive oil
- 1 rib celery, diced
- 2 medium carrots, peeled and diced
- 1 small onion, diced
- 3 cups water, divided
- 1 package ramen noodles, beef flavor
- 1/2 cup green lentils
- Salt and pepper
- Grated Parmesan cheese, for garnish

Instructions:

In a pan, heat the oil. Add in the onion, celery, and carrots, and sauté, stirring occasionally, for about 7 minutes.

Stir in 2 cups water, the ramen seasoning, and the lentils. Bring to a boil, then cover partially so that just a crack remains. Reduce the heat and cook until lentils are soft, about 20 minutes.

Add the remaining 1 cup of water and bring to a simmer over medium heat. Break the ramen noodles into 4 to 6 pieces and add them to the soup. Simmer until the noodles are tender, about 4 minutes. Season to taste with salt and pepper. Serve with Parmesan cheese sprinkled on top.

4. Brown Sauce Noodles

As if there weren't enough arguments over whether it was the Italians or the Chinese who invented noodles (they both did), we are now getting into who invented the Bolognese sauce as well. Here, it is brown bean instead of tomato and pork instead of veal, but we can still feel gratitude for having both in the world.

Time: 20m

Serves: 4

Ingredients:

- 4 tbsp brown bean sauce
- 1 tbsp hoisin sauce
- ½ cup chicken stock
- ½ tsp sugar
- 2 tbsp peanut or corn oil
- 5 spring onions, white part, chopped
- 1 tbsp finely chopped garlic
- 1 lb. minced pork
- 14 oz fresh Shanghai noodles
- 1 cucumber, cut into long matchsticks
- 2 spring onions, green part, finely sliced
- 1 cup bean sprouts, blanched

Instructions:

Mash brown bean sauce with the back of a spoon and mix well with hoisin sauce, stock and sugar.

In a wok, fry spring onion and garlic for 20 seconds. Add pork and stir fry until it separates into small pieces and is coloured, about 2 to 3 minutes. Add the bean mixture, reduce heat and simmer for 5 minutes.

Boil water and cook noodles for 4 to 5 minutes. Drain and place in a large bowl. Spoon the brown sauce over them and arrange a sheaf of cucumber strips on top. Serve with more cucumber strips, spring onion greens and bean sprouts, so that everyone can help themselves, folding the goodies through the sauce and the noodles.

5. Egg Flower Noodle Soup

This is a serious version of good old chicken and sweet corn soup, but without the chicken and the sweet corn.

Time: 1h

Serves: 4

Ingredients:

- 10 oz. pork belly
- ¼ cup dried wood fungus
- 8 dried shiitake mushrooms
- 2 tbsp peanut oil
- 1 tbsp minced fresh ginger
- 3 spring onions, green part only, finely sliced
- ½ cup bamboo shoots, cut into matchsticks
- 4 cups chicken stock
- 1 tsp salt
- 2 tbsp soy sauce
- 1 tbsp shaohsing rice wine or dry sherry
- 11 oz. fresh flat egg noodles
- ½ cup ham, sliced into thin strips
- 1 tbsp cornstarch, mixed with 1 tbsp water
- 2 eggs, beaten
- 1 tsp sesame oil
- ½ tsp pepper

Instructions:

Put pork belly in a saucepan, cover with cold water and bring to the boil. Skim off any nasty stuff, reduce heat and simmer for 45 minutes. Turn off the heat and leave pork in the liquid to cool.

Soak the wood fungus and mushrooms separately in hot water for about an hour. Drain and rinse well, then cut into thin strips, discarding any stems.

Cut the cooled pork into thin strips about 1 in wide (reserve the cooking liquid, skimming off the fat).

Heat peanut oil in a saucepan and cook ginger, mushrooms, wood fungus and bamboo shoots and stir fry briefly. Add chicken stock and 4 cups of the pork cooking liquid and bring to the boil. Add salt, soy sauce and rice wine, taste, adjust seasonings, and simmer for 3 minutes.

Cook noodles in boiling water for about 1 minute. Drain, rinse in cold water and drain again. Return to the saucepan, off the heat, and keep warm.

Add pork and ham to the soup, turn up the heat and stir in the cornstarch mixture. Stir until the soup thickens, lower heat and slowly pour the egg into the soup in a thin stream through the tines of a fork. Stir lightly, then add sesame oil and pepper. Divide noodles between 4 bowls. Ladle soup over and scatter with spring onions.

6. Chiu Chow Dessert Noodles

This wonderfully simple dish is sweet and sour in its most sublime form.

Time: 20m

Serves: 4

Ingredients:

- 3 oz dried egg noodles
- 2 tbsp peanut oil
- 3 tbsp Chinese red vinegar
- 3 tbsp white sugar

Instructions:

Put noodles in a pot of boiling water and simmer for 3 minutes, or until tender. Rinse under cold, running water and drain thoroughly. Set aside for 2 hours, then pat dry.

Heat oil in a hot wok and swirl around to cover the surface. Put noodles in the wok and flatten them against the surface, pressing them with the back of a ladle. Cook for about 5 minutes, until golden and crisp on the underside. Place a large plate on top of the wok and invert the wok so that the flat noodle pancake tips out onto the plate. Slide the pancake back in and cook on the other side.

Cut pancake into 4. Serve with side bowls of red vinegar and white sugar. Sprinkle both on top, to your own taste, and eat with chopsticks or fork and spoon.

7. Beef and Water Spinach Noodles

Water spinach, known as ong choy in Cantonese, is a seductive, velvety vegetable that adds a little touch of luxury to anything it comes near. Here it turns a homely bowl of beef noodles into something with real depth and character.

Time: 2h

Serves: 4

Ingredients:

- 7 oz beef (scotch fillet or rump)
- 1 tbsp cornstarch
- 3 tbsp soy sauce
- 1 tsp sugar
- 1 tsp shaohsing rice wine, or dry sherry
- 4 tbsp peanut oil
- 10 oz dried wheat noodles
- 14 oz water spinach (ong choy), thoroughly washed
- 2 spring onions, finely sliced
- 1 tbsp ginger, grated
- 2 cloves of garlic, finely chopped
- 1 tbsp hoisin sauce
- 2 tbsp chicken stock
- ½ tsp salt
- pinch of black pepper

Instructions:

Finely slice meat into thin strips 2 in long. Rub cornstarch into the meat, combine with 1 tablespoon soy sauce, the sugar, rice wine and 1 tablespoon oil, and leave to marinate for an hour

Cook noodles in plenty of salted, boiling water for about 4 minutes, or until tender, then rinse well under cold water, drain and set aside.

Cut water spinach into 6 in (2½ in) pieces.

Heat 2 tablespoons oil in a hot wok and stir fry water spinach for a minute or two, moving continuously. Remove spinach, set aside and add 1 more tablespoon of oil to the wok. Stir fry beef for 1 minute, add half the spring onion, the ginger, garlic and hoisin sauce and stir fry for another minute over high heat. Add remaining 2 tablespoons soy sauce, stock, salt and black pepper. When the liquid starts to boil, add the noodles and water spinach and heat through, stirring well to combine. Sprinkle with spring onion and serve.

8. Chicken Noodle Soup

Real chicken noodle soup is made from real chicken stock, with real chicken pieces and the freshest egg noodles you can lay your hands on.

Time: 30m

Serves: 4

Ingredients:

- 1 tsp salt
- 1 egg white, lightly beaten
- 2 tsp cornstarch
- 2 chicken breasts, cut into thin strips
- 8 dried shiitake mushrooms, soaked
- 11 oz fresh flat egg noodles
- 1 tbsp peanut oil
- 3 oz bamboo shoots, cut into thin matchsticks
- ½ bunch choy sum (flowering cabbage) leaves, roughly chopped
- 3 spring onions, cut into 1 in lengths
- 2 tbsp light soy sauce
- 1 tbsp shaohsing rice wine, or dry sherry
- 1 tsp sugar
- 1 tsp sesame oil
- 8 cups chicken stock, simmering

Instructions:

Combine ½ teaspoon of salt, egg white and cornstarch in a bowl, add chicken and toss to coat. Leave for 20 minutes to 'velvet' the chicken. Drain mushrooms, remove stems and slice caps finely.

Cook noodles in boiling water for 2 minutes, rinse in cold water and drain well.

Heat oil in a hot wok and stir fry chicken, bamboo shoots and mushrooms for 2 minutes. Add choy sum and spring onion and stir fry for another minute. Add soy sauce, rice wine, sugar, sesame oil and ½ teaspoon salt.

Add noodles to the stock and return to the boil. Add the contents of the wok, stir through and serve in Chinese bowls with soup spoons and chopsticks.

9. Long-Life Noodles

No celebration or banquet is complete without a dish of long-life noodles, served either at the beginning or the very end. The idea is simple: the longer the noodle, the longer you will live!

Time: 15m

Ingredients:

- 4 spring onions
- 8 dried shiitake mushrooms, soaked
- 1 large e-fu noodle cake, about 11 oz
- 2 tbsp soy sauce
- 1 tbsp oyster sauce
- 1 tsp sesame oil
- 1 tsp sugar
- ¾ cup chicken stock
- 1 tbsp peanut oil
- 1 tbsp grated ginger
- 2 cloves of garlic, crushed with the side of a knife blade

Instructions:

Finely slice the green tops of the spring onions and reserve. Cut the remainder into matchsticks. Drain mushrooms, discard stems and slice caps finely.

Cook noodle in boiling water for 3 to 4 minutes. Rinse in cold water and drain well.

Mix soy sauce, oyster sauce, sesame oil, sugar and chicken stock in a bowl and set aside.

Heat peanut oil in a hot wok and stir fry ginger and garlic for 1 minute. Add spring onion matchsticks, all of the mushrooms and sauce ingredients and bring to the boil, stirring. Cook for 1 minute. Add noodles and cook for about 2 minutes, or until they have absorbed most of the sauce. Serve immediately, scattered with the spring onion greens.

10. Roast Pork Noodle Soup

No self–respecting noodle lover should ever live more than a short drive from a Chinese barbecued meats shop. Of course, you can make your own char sieu and keep it in the fridge, but that way, you can't pick up a piece of suckling pig and a little white cut chicken at the same time.

Time: 30m

Serves: 4

Ingredients:

- 7 oz dried wheat noodles
- ½ bunch gai laan (Chinese broccoli) about 11 oz
- 3 tbsp peanut oil
- 6 slices of ginger, cut into matchsticks
- 1 tbsp shaohsing rice wine, or dry sherry
- 2 tbsp oyster sauce
- 2 tbsp soy sauce
- ½ tsp salt
- pinch of black pepper
- 2 tsp sugar
- ½ tsp sesame oil
- 1 tbsp cornstarch, mixed with a little water
- 7 oz char sieu (red roast pork), cut into thin slices
- 2 spring onions, sliced on the diagonal into 1 inch lengths
- 8 cups chicken stock
- 1 spring onion, green part only, sliced into 1 inch lengths

Instructions:

Cook noodles in plenty of salted, boiling water for 4 minutes, or until tender, then rinse well under cold water, drain and set aside.

Cut gai laan into 2½ pieces. Put thick stems in a pot of boiling water and cook for 1 minute. Add leaves and thinner stems and cook for 20 seconds. Remove from pot and plunge into cold water. When cool, drain and set aside.

Heat peanut oil and stir fry ginger for 60 seconds, add gai laan and stir fry for another minute. Add rice wine, oyster sauce, soy sauce, salt, pepper, sugar, sesame oil and cornstarch mixture. When liquid starts to boil, add pork and spring onion and heat through, stirring.

In a separate pot, bring chicken stock to the boil. Put noodles in a strainer or colander and pour boiling water over the top to warm them. Drain well. To serve, put a handful of noodles into each of 4 bowls. Pour chicken stock over noodles and top with pork mixture. Scatter spring onion on top and serve with spoons and chopsticks.

11. Two-Sides-Brown Noodles with Shredded Duck

It may seem something of a pointless exercise, creating a crisp, crunchy noodle pancake just so you can pour sauce all over it, and make the noodles go soggy again. But that is exactly the point. If you don't get it now, you will with your first mouthful.

Serves: 4

Time: 20m

Ingredients:

- 7 oz dried wheat noodles (thin)
- 4 tbsp peanut oil
- 2 cloves of garlic, crushed with the side of a knife blade
- 2 slices fresh ginger
- 1 bunch choy sum (flowering cabbage), cut into 2 inch sections
- 6 shiitake mushrooms, soaked for 1 hour, and sliced
- 3 bamboo shoots, cut into matchsticks
- 8 water chestnuts, sliced thinly
- 1 lup cheong sausage, cut into matchsticks
- meat from ½ Chinese roast duck, sliced finely
- 1 cup bean sprouts, rinsed
- 1 tbsp oyster sauce
- 1 tbsp soy sauce
- ½ cup chicken stock
- 1 tsp cornstarch
- 1 tbsp shaohsing rice wine, or dry sherry
- 3 spring onions, finely sliced

Instructions:

Drop noodles into a pot of boiling water and cook for about 4 minutes. Rinse under cold water and drain well.

Heat 2 tablespoons peanut oil in a hot wok and cook 1 clove of garlic and 1 slice of ginger for a minute to flavour the oil, then remove. Add thicker choy sum stems and stir fry for 2 minutes. Add mushroom, bamboo shoot, water chestnuts, lup cheong and duck and stir fry for 2 minutes. Add choy sum leaves and bean sprouts and stir fry until they soften. Add oyster sauce, soy sauce and stock and toss lightly. Mix cornstarch with rice wine and stir into the mixture. Tip everything into a heatproof bowl and keep warm in a low oven.

Heat remaining peanut oil in a hot wok and cook remaining ginger and garlic for 1 minute until golden, then discard. Tip noodles into wok and flatten them against the surface. Cook for 4 to 5 minutes until golden brown. Place a flat plate on top of the wok and invert the whole thing so that the noodle pancake falls onto the plate. Return wok to heat, add a little extra oil, slide pancake back in and cook the other side. Turn out on a large, warmed serving platter and top with stir-fried mixture and spring onion.

12. Buddhist Vegetable Noodles

This recipe is based on a classic Buddhist vegetarian dish that manages to satisfy both aesthetically and gastronomically.

Time: 20m

Ingredients:

- 4 tbsp peanut oil
- 1 small onion, sliced lengthwise
- 2 slices ginger, finely chopped
- 8 dried shiitake mushrooms, soaked and sliced (reserve soaking water)
- 2 cloves of garlic, finely chopped
- 1 tbsp vegetarian oyster sauce
- 3 tbsp light soy sauce
- ½ red capsicum, thinly sliced ½ green capsicum, thinly sliced
- ½ medium carrot, thinly sliced
- 3 tbsp bamboo shoots, cut into matchsticks
- 2 cups shredded Tientsin cabbage
- 1 cup bean sprouts, rinsed
- ½ tsp salt
- pinch of white pepper
- ½ tsp sugar
- 2 tsp sesame oil
- 1 tbsp shaohsing rice wine, or dry sherry
- 10 oz fresh egg noodles
- 1 tsp peanut oil
- 2 spring onions, green part only, finely sliced

Instructions:

Heat 1 tablespoon oil in a hot wok and stir fry onion until translucent. Add ginger, mushrooms, garlic and cook for another minute. Add the oyster sauce and 2 tablespoons soy sauce and cook for another 30 seconds. Transfer wok contents to a bowl. Heat 2 tablespoons oil in the wok and stir fry capsicum, carrot, bamboo shoots and cabbage for 3 minutes on high heat. Add bean sprouts, salt, pepper, sugar and 4 tablespoons reserved mushroom water, and cook for 1 minute. Add onion and mushroom mixture, sesame oil and rice wine and combine well.

Cook noodles in plenty of water at a rolling boil for about 1 minute. Thoroughly drain, rinse under the cold running water, and drain well. Toss with remaining 1 tablespoon soy sauce and 1 teaspoon oil. Put noodles on a large warmed serving platter, spoon on vegetable mixture and mix lightly. Sprinkle with spring onion and serve.

13. Noodles with Shredded Lamb

This simple dish combines lamb and noodles in an easy, ingenious way that even a Cantonese could learn to love.

Time: 30m

Serves: 4

Ingredients:

- 7 oz. vermicelli
- 7 oz. lamb fillet, cut into thin pieces
- 1 beaten egg
- 1 tbsp. cornstarch
- ½ tsp. salt
- 2 tbsp. water
- 2 tbsp. peanut oil
- 3 tbsp. soy sauce
- 3 spring onions, green only, cut into 2 in lengths
- 1 cup chicken stock
- 1 tsp. sesame oil
- 2 tbsp. rice wine, or dry sherry

Instructions:

Place noodles in a large bowl and add boiling water. Allow to stand for 4 minutes. Drain.

Combine egg, cornstarch, salt and water in a bowl. Coat lamb and leave aside for 10 to 15 minutes.

In a large wok, heat peanut oil and stir fry lamb for 1 or 2 minutes. Add soy and spring onion. Add stock, noodles, sesame oil and rice wine and cook for another couple of minutes. Serve warm!

14. Hokkien Noodles with Prawns

This is an intriguing, 'soft' combination of flavour and texture, lit up by the surprising, gentle Shanghainese sweetness that comes from the sugar and the ketchup.

Time: 30m

Serves: 4

Ingredients:

- 1 lb. Hokkien noodles
- 7 oz small raw prawns, peeled
- ½ tsp salt
- 3 tsp cornstarch
- 7 oz pork loin
- 3 tbsp soy sauce
- 4 tbsp peanut oil
- 2 small onions (or 4 shallots), finely sliced
- ¾ cup chicken stock
- 1 tbsp tomato sauce (ketchup)
- 1 tbsp sugar
- 1 tsp sesame oil

Ingredients:

Put noodles in a heatproof bowl, cover with boiling water and leave for 1 minute. Drain well and set aside. Mix prawns with a pinch of salt and 1 teaspoon cornstarch. Cut pork into thin strips and mix with 1 tablespoon soy sauce and 1 teaspoon cornstarch and leave to stand for 20 minutes.

Heat 2 tablespoons oil in a hot wok and stir fry prawns quickly for 1 minute. Remove from wok. Add another tablespoon of oil and stir fry pork for about 2 minutes. Remove from wok. Add 1 tablespoon of oil and cook onion until soft. Add 2 tablespoons soy sauce, the stock, salt to taste, tomato ketchup, sugar and sesame oil.

Bring to the boil, add noodles and cook for 1 to 2 minutes. Return pork and prawns to the hot wok and toss well. Mix remaining teaspoon of cornstarch with a teaspoon of water and stir through until the sauce thickens slightly. Serve on a warm platter or in small Chinese bowls.

15. Bang Bang Chicken Noodles

Traditionally, this popular dish from northern China – of poached chicken in a nutty, sweet, chilli sauce – doesn't include noodles. Yet the subtle crunch of the bean thread vermicelli adds substance and character and lightens a meat–heavy dish.

Time: 20m

Serves: 4

Ingredients:

- 7 oz bean thread vermicelli
- 2 tsp sesame oil
- 1 chicken, about 2 ½ lb.
- 2 spring onions, green part only, finely sliced

Sauce

- 1 tsp sesame seeds
- 2½ tbsp Chinese sesame paste or smooth peanut butter
- 1 tbsp chilli bean sauce
- 2 tbsp cooked peanut oil (heated, then cooled)
- 2 tsp sesame oil
- 1 tbsp sugar
- 1 tbsp soy sauce
- 1½ tbsp Chinese black vinegar
- 2 tbsp chicken stock

Instructions:

Pour boiling water over noodles in a heatproof bowl and let stand for 3 to 5 minutes. Drain. Cut noodles roughly with a pair of scissors and toss with 1 teaspoon sesame oil.

Lightly toast sesame seeds in a dry, hot pan.

Make sauce by combining sesame paste, chilli bean sauce, cooked peanut oil and sesame oil until it forms a paste. Stir in sugar, soy sauce, black vinegar and chicken stock, and sprinkle sesame seeds on top. Set aside.

Put chicken in a saucepan with a snug–fitting lid and just cover with cold water. Remove chicken and bring water to the boil. Return chicken to the water, reduce heat until water is barely simmering, and cover tightly. Simmer for 30 minutes.

Remove chicken from the saucepan and plunge into a large bowl of icy–cold water. Lift out and replunge three or four times, which will give the chicken a marvelously smooth texture. Brush chicken with remaining teaspoon sesame oil. Remove chicken meat from bones and shred finely.

Put noodles on a large serving plate. Arrange shredded chicken on top, and pour on the sauce, serving any extra sauce in a small bowl for dipping. Scatter with spring onion and serve.

16. Chicken Noodle Salad

This is a glorious celebration of fresh, wild, garden smells, laced with the heady fragrance of sesame and ginger. It is important to use the chicken soon after it has been cooked. If it has been refrigerated, it will lose much of its lusciousness and bounce, thus losing the point of the whole exercise.

Time: 15m

Serves: 4

Ingredients:

- 10 oz dried rice vermicelli
- 1 tbsp sesame oil
- 1 white cut (poached) chicken (from Chinese barbecued meats shop)
- 1 cucumber
- 1 small bunch coriander

Dressing

- 1 bunch spring onions
- 8 tbsp peanut oil
- 2 tbsp shredded fresh ginger
- 1 tsp salt

Instructions:

Boil water and pour over noodles and leave to stand for 6 to 7 minutes. In a separate saucepan, boil more water as you wait. Drain noodles and transfer to boiling water. Cook for 60 seconds.

Rinse in cold water and drain thoroughly. Chop noodles roughly a couple of times with scissors. Add sesame oil and toss thoroughly. Cover and set aside.

Remove meat from the chicken and slice finely, discarding skin and bones.

Peel cucumber, cut in half lengthwise and scoop out seeds with a teaspoon. Slice cucumber flesh lengthwise and cut each slice into thin matchsticks. Pick leaves from coriander and set aside.

To make spring onion dressing, finely chop green parts of the spring onions. Gently warm peanut oil in a wok, then add ginger and salt. Stir briefly until salt dissolves, add spring onion and stir for 10 to 15 seconds, until it starts to soften. Remove from heat.

In a bowl, combine chicken, cucumber, noodles, coriander and half the warm dressing. Top with the rest of the dressing.

17. Thai Shrimp Noodle Soup

This delicious Thai noodle soup is super delicious and easy to make! The best part? It's pretty healthy too!

Preparation Time: 20 minutes

Cooking Time: 15 minutes

Servings: 2

Ingredients

- 3 tbsp. peeled and very thinly slivered fresh ginger
- 10 oz. medium-size shrimp, peeled and deveined
- 2 ½ tbsp. fish sauce or soy sauce
- 3 carrots, thinly sliced
- 2 cloves garlic, finely minced
- 2 tsp chopped fresh basil
- 3 cups coarsely chopped fresh spinach
- 10 cups water
- 3 packets of chicken flavored Ramen noodles
- 4 green onions, minced
- 2 tbsp. Thai hot chili sauce
- 1 cup sliced mushrooms
- Juice and grated zest from 1 ½ limes

Instructions:

Fill a large pot with water. Bring this water to a boil on a high flame.

Add the carrots, fish sauce, green onions, ginger, garlic, basil and chili sauce.

Break the noodles and put them into the water as well. Keep stirring to separate the strands.

Now add the seasoning from 2 packets that came with the noodles. Boil for 5 minutes or so.

After this, add the shrimp, mushrooms and spinach. Cook for another 5 minutes.

Top with lime zest and juice and stir well.

18. Cranberry Nectarine Salad

Like cranberries? You'll love this cranberry salad!

Preparation Time: 5 minutes

Cooking Time: 20 minutes

Servings: 3

Ingredients

- Two 3 oz. packets of Ramen noodles
- 1 ½ tbsp. soy sauce
- 1 packet of gourmet mixed salad greens (wash them thoroughly)
- 2 tbsp. light brown sugar
- 1 tbsp. balsamic vinegar
- 1 cup dried cranberries
- 2 cups hot water
- ½ cup canola oil
- 1 ½ tbsp. rice wine vinegar
- 2 large nectarines, peeled and cut in wedges
- 1 cup coarsely chopped walnuts
- 10 oz. crumbled feta cheese

Directions

Preheat the oven to 350 degrees Fahrenheit.

Keep the packets of seasoning that come with the soup mix aside. Break the noodles into smaller pieces and place them in a pan. Make sure that they are as spread out as possible.

Put this pan in the oven. Bake at the same temperature for around 6 minutes. Remove the pan when the noodles are toasted. Stir them occasionally so that the heat is evenly spread out.

After this, place the pan aside to cool the noodles down.

In a small bowl, pour the cranberries. Heat some water (not boil) and add this to the cranberries. Leave the cranberries in the water for some time and then drain the water.

In another large bowl, whisk the contents from the seasoning packet with the canola oil and the four ingredients that follow from the list above.

Add the cranberries, gourmet greens, Ramen noodles and the rest of the ingredients to this bowl. Toss the contents in order to mix well. Serve when hot.

19. Vegetable Primavera

Using frozen veggies cuts the time consumed in half with this easy recipe!

Preparation Time: 10 minutes

Cooking Time: 15 minutes

Servings: 2

Ingredients

- 1 ½ bags of frozen mixed vegetables like asparagus, carrots, cauliflower and broccoli
- 4 packets of Ramen noodle soup. The flavor can be anything
- 3 cups water
- 2 packets of French onion spreadable cheese
- 1 jar of pimientos (sliced)

Instructions:

Take a clean and dry pot. Add the 3 cups water to this and bring it to a boil. Now add the frozen vegetables and bring it back to a boil.

Now break the blocks of noodles and add them to the water as well. Keep stirring and let the contents cook for around 3 minutes until the vegetables become tender.

Drain the contents using a colander.

Place the pot on a medium heat now. Add some more water and the seasoning packets. Add the cheese to the pot as well. Keep stirring until you obtain a smooth mixture.

Add all ingredients and cook for around 5 minutes. Serve hot.

20. Eight Treasure Noodles

To the Chinese, eight is a significant and lucky number because the word for eight sounds very much like the word for prosperous. For this reason, celebratory banquets will often officially consist of eight courses (even if a few extras are thrown in for good measure). In Chinese cooking, there is eight treasure duck, eight treasure chicken and eight treasure rice. Today we try eight treasure noodles.

Time: 20m

Serves: 4

Ingredients:

- 3 tbsp dried shrimp, soaked for 30 minutes
- 6 dried shiitake mushrooms, soaked
- 2 tbsp peanut oil
- 2 cup cheong sausages, thinly sliced
- ½ cup lotus seeds or gingko nuts (available canned)
- ½ onion, finely diced
- ½ cup bamboo shoots, cut into matchsticks
- 2 tbsp dark soy sauce
- ½ tsp five spice powder
- 2 tsp sesame oil
- 1 tsp salt
- 3 oz char sieu (red roast pork), cut into thin strips
- 1 cooked chicken thigh, cut into thin strips
- 1 cup chicken stock
- 1 tsp cornstarch
- 1 tbsp shaohsing rice wine
- 11 oz dried wheat noodles
- 2 spring onions, green part only, finely sliced

Instructions:

Drain dried shrimp and mushrooms. Stem mushrooms and slice caps finely. Heat peanut oil and stir fry shrimp, mushroom, sausage, lotus seeds, onion and bamboo shoots for 2 minutes. Add soy sauce, five spice powder, sesame oil and salt.

Add pork, chicken and chicken stock and cook, stirring, for 1 minute. Mix cornstarch into rice wine and stir into the mixture. Cook for 1 minute until sauce thickens slightly.

Meanwhile, cook noodles in plenty of boiling water for 3 to 4 minutes. Drain and combine with the sauce, tossing well. Serve on a large warmed platter or in small Chinese bowls with spring onion scattered over the top.

21. San Choy Bau with Cellophane Noodles

With its minced meat, water chestnuts, mushrooms and bamboo shoots inside a crisp, fresh lettuce leaf, san choy bau manages to roll up all the principles of Chinese cooking in one neat little parcel.

Time: 15m

Makes: 8

Ingredients:

- 2 oz bean thread vermicelli
- 2 fresh quails
- 6 dried shiitake mushrooms, soaked
- 3 tbsp peanut oil
- 2 slices ginger, finely chopped
- 7 oz bamboo shoots, finely chopped
- 1 clove of garlic, finely chopped
- 6 water chestnuts, finely chopped
- 5 oz minced pork or chicken
- 1 slice leg ham, diced
- 1 tsp sugar
- ½ tsp salt
- pinch of white pepper
- 1 tbsp dark soy sauce
- 1 tbsp hoisin sauce
- 1 tbsp dry sherry
- 2 tbsp chicken stock
- 1:1 miture of cornstarch and water (1 tsp each)
- ½ tsp sesame oil
- 8 perfect lettuce leaves, washed and dried

Instructions:

Put noodles in a heatproof bowl and pour boiling water over to cover. Leave for 3 to 4 minutes.

Drain and rinse under cold water. With a pair of scissors, cut into roughly 2 inch lengths.

Remove meat from quails, chop finely and set aside.

Drain mushrooms, stem, and finely slice caps. Heat oil and stir fry mushrooms and ginger for 1 minute. Add bamboo shoots, garlic and water chestnuts and stir fry for 30 seconds. Add quail meat, pork or chicken, ham, sugar, salt and pepper and stir fry over high heat for 3 minutes. Add noodles, soy sauce, hoisin sauce, rice wine, chicken stock and cornstarch mixture and cook for another 60 seconds or until it starts to thicken. Sprinkle sesame oil on top, spoon into lettuce cups and serve. To eat, roll up the cup and eat with your fingers.

22. Suckling Pig, Jellyfish and Noodle Salad

Without the noodles, this traditional banquet dish is texture city, running from the sharp crack of the pig skin, to the India rubber chew of the jellyfish and the satisfying crunch of cucumber and celery. With the noodles, it takes on even more bounce.

Time: 20m

Serves: 4

Ingredients:

- 7 oz dried jellyfish
- 5 oz bean thread vermicelli
- 1 tbsp sesame oil
- 2 spring onions, green part only
- ½ cucumber, peeled
- 1 carrot, peeled
- 2 stalks of celery
- 14 oz cooked suckling pig (from Chinese barbecued meats shop)
- 1 tbsp soy sauce
- 1 tbsp white vinegar
- 1 tsp sugar

Instructions:

Soak jellyfish in a large pot of water for 24 hours, changing the water 3 or 4 times. Trim each piece of jellyfish then roll up like a piece of carpet. Trim edges and cut into strips about ½ in wide. Dip strips in boiling water, drain and let cool. Pat dry with paper towels.

Pour boiling water over noodles in a heatproof bowl, let stand for 3 to 5 minutes and drain. Mix with sesame oil and set aside.

Cut 1 spring onion into 2 in sections, then cut each section into matchsticks and set aside.

Using a tsp, scoop and discard seeds from the cucumber. Cut cucumber, carrot and celery into fine matchsticks. Remove skin from suckling pig and cut into thin shards. Cut flesh into thin strips and toss lightly through the jellyfish with the cucumber, carrot, celery and noodles. Add soy sauce, vinegar, sugar and remaining spring onion, finely chopped, and toss again. Serve on a large, warmed serving platter and scatter the crisp skin over the top.

23. Spring Rain Tempura

Harusame, also known as 'spring rain', are usually served in salads and soups, but they also have the ability to puff up quite dramatically when deep fried. This unusual tempura recipe makes the most of that ability, giving the seafood an almost theatrical appearance.

Time: 20m

Serves:

Ingredients:

- 14 oz white fish fillets
- 12 medium-size prawns
- 2 green capsicums
- 4 oz plain flour
- 2 egg whites
- 3 oz harusame
- vegetable oil, for deep frying

Dipping sauce

- 1 cup dashi
- 1/3 cup mirin
- 1/3 cup light soy sauce
- 2 tbsp grated daikon (white radish)

Instructions:

Cut fish into 6 in long pieces. Devein prawns by hooking out the black intestinal tract with a fine bamboo skewer. Cut capsicum lengthwise into 1 in strips. Put flour in a shallow bowl. Add egg whites and beat until frothy, but not stiff and peaky. Put noodles in a large plastic bag and cut into ½ in lengths inside the bag.

To make dipping sauce, combine dashi, mirin and soy sauce in a small saucepan and bring to the boil. Remove from heat. Pour into individual bowls, adding a little of the grated daikon.

Pour enough oil for deep frying into a hot wok or saucepan and heat until a cube of bread dances on the surface, turning golden within 5 seconds. Roll prawns, fish and capsicum strips first in flour, then in egg white, then in harusame noodles. Drop pieces of coated fish or prawns into the oil, 3 at a time. The noodles will puff out dramatically. Fry until fish or prawns are cooked and noodles are pale gold. Remove and drain well. Continue the process until all seafood and vegetable pieces are fried. (Whisk the egg white briskly before each dipping to keep it frothy.)

Arrange seafood and vegetables on small serving platters and serve with dipping sauce.

24. Chilled Somen

An exceptionally refreshing summer dish, this is the zen of cold noodles in a single bowl – pared-back, subtle, yet with intriguing and satisfying layers of flavour. Resist the temptation to overcook the noodles, as they need to retain an almost al dente bite to keep up the diner's interest.

Time: 15m

Serves:

Ingredients:

- 7 oz somen
- 6 dried shiitake mushrooms
- 1½ cups dashi
- ½ cup mirin
- 5 tbsp soy sauce
- 1 small cucumber, cut into matchsticks
- 1 handful of watercress, blanched
- 2 spring onions, finely chopped
- 1 tsp prepared wasabi

Instructions:

Add noodles to boiling water. When water returns to the boil, add ½ cup cold water.

Allow to boil again and add another ½ cup of cold water.

Allow to cook for 2 minutes then rinse and drain. Chill for about 2 hours.

Soak mushrooms in hot water for an hour, then drain and cut off stems.

To make the dipping sauce, combine dashi, mirin, soy sauce and mushrooms in a saucepan and simmer for 5 minutes. Remove mushrooms and cut in half.

Strain liquid and cool quickly by pouring it into bowl sitting in another bowl filled with iced water. Refrigerate until well-chilled.

Divide noodles among 4 Japanese plates or bowls and top with cucumber strips, a little mound of watercress, 2 mushroom halves and spring onions. Serve with dipping sauce and wasabi.

25. Curry Udon

The Japanese have adopted the idea of curry in much the same way they adopted the art of deep frying from the Portuguese, and the art of crumbing from eastern Europe. Curry powder first came to Japan in the late 19th century and, while in no way resembling Indian cookery, Japanese curries have a peculiar charm all their own.

Time: 20m

Serves: 4

Ingredients:

- 10 oz dried udon
- 2 tbsp peanut oil
- 2 onions, sliced
- 11 oz boned, chicken thigh, cut into bite-size cubes
- 1 cup green beans, blanched
- 2 tsp curry powder
- 4 cups chicken stock
- 1 tsp sugar
- 2 tbsp tapioca starch or potato starch
- 2 spring onions, finely sliced

Instructions:

Boil water and add noodles. When the water returns to the boil, add 1 cup cold water. When water again returns to the boil, add another cup cold water. Repeat the process another 2 to 4 times, depending on thickness of udon, until the noodles are cooked but still have a little resilience. Drain, rinse in cold water and set aside.

Heat oil and fry onion gently for a couple of minutes. Add chicken and cook for 1 minute, then add beans and cook for another minute. Sprinkle on curry powder and mix in with a wooden spoon. Pour in stock and sugar, bring to the boil and simmer for 3 minutes. Mix tapioca starch with a little water. Drizzle mixture into the pot, stirring thoroughly. Cook until it begins to boil and starts to thicken.

Pour boiling water over noodles in a colander or strainer in the sink. Drain well and distribute warmed noodles among 4 individual bowls. Pour sauce over noodles and scatter with spring onion.

26. Moon-Viewing Noodles

Of course that's not a mysterious moon drifting meaningfully through the clouds. It's a raw egg. If you can see the beauty in that, too, then you're ready to appreciate tsukimi udon, which is a great favourite in a country where moon-viewing is a popular family pastime.

Time: 10m

Ingredients:

- 14 oz fresh, cooked, or instant udon
- 6 cups dashi
- 1 tablespoon mirin
- 2 tablespoons light soy sauce
- 4 fresh eggs
- 8 slices kamaboko (fish cake)
- 4 dried shiitake mushrooms, soaked, stemed, caps sliced in half
- ½ sheet nori (seaweed)
- 2 large spring onions, sliced thinly on the diagonal

Instructions:

Boil water and pour over noodles. Gently separate them with chopsticks. Drain and rinse under cold water.

Bring dashi to the boil in a saucepan with mirin and soy sauce and simmer for 3 minutes. Reheat noodles briefly in boiling water, then divide among 4 warmed serving bowls, making a little hollow nest in each pile.

Add boiling stock to come halfway up the noodles, then break an egg into each nest. Arrange fish cake and mushroom to one side and carefully ladle more boiling soup on top to just cover the egg. Immediately cover each bowl with a plate and leave for 2 minutes before removing it.

If you're not sure about eating a very lightly set egg, poach the eggs separately to your liking and slip them in at the last moment. Toast nori over a gas flame for a few seconds until it crisps. Cut into thin strips and scatter over the top, along with the spring onion.

27. Penang Laksa

When most people think of laksa, they think of curry laksa, or laksa lemak. But the people of Penang have devised their own laksa using fish. Rather than thick, creamy and coconutty, this laksa is sour and brothy – a totally different kettle of fish.

Time: 20m

Serves: 4

Ingredients:

- 4 cups cold water
- ½ tsp salt
- 1 lb. blue mackerel, or other firm-fleshed fish
- 2 cups tamarind water
- 2 stalks of lemongrass, white part only, finely sliced
- 2 tsp ground turmeric
- 1 tbsp belacan (shrimp paste)
- 6 dried chillies, soaked, drained and chopped
- ¾ inch piece galangal or ginger, finely chopped
- 1 tbsp palm sugar, or white sugar
- 10 oz round rice noodles or Hokkien noodles
- 1 cucumber, peeled, and cut into thin matchsticks

Ingredients:

Bring water and salt to the boil, add fish and simmer for 5 minutes. Remove fish, cool, then flake off flesh with your hands and set aside. Return heads and bones to the water. Add tamarind water and simmer for a further 10 minutes, then strain through a fine sieve and set stock aside.

Pound or blend lemongrass, turmeric, belacan, chilli and galangal to a paste. Add to fish stock with sugar and simmer for 10 minutes. Add fish and heat through.

Pour boiling water over noodles in a heatproof bowl. Drain and divide noodles among 4 warm serving bowls. Add soup and top with cucumber.

28. Singapore Beehoon

Singapore noodles, or Sing chow, is widely known outside the Lion City, but unheard of in its home town. More usually it is simply called fried beehoon, after the noodle itself. The popular addition of curry powder is not to my taste, but feel free to add a teaspoon worth of good, fresh Malaysian curry powder if it is to yours.

Time: 20m

Serves: 4

Ingredients:

- 8 oz rice vermicelli
- 1 tbsp vegetable oil
- ½ onion, or 4 shallots, sliced
- 1 egg, lightly beaten
- 1 tbsp chicken stock or water
- 3 oz cooked shredded chicken
- 3 oz char sieu (red roast pork), sliced
- 1 tbsp dark soy sauce
- 1 tbsp light soy sauce
- 5 oz prawns, shelled
- ½ cup bean sprouts
- 2 spring onions, finely chopped
- ½ cup shredded lettuce
- 1 tbsp crisp-fried shallots (available from Asian grocery stores)
- 1 lemon, quartered

Instructions:

Pour boiling water over noodles in a heatproof bowl and let stand for 6 to 7 minutes. Rinse in cold water and drain.

In a wok, fry onions in hot oil until it starts to soften. Add egg and stir until softly cooked. Add drained noodles and stir constantly to coat with egg. Moisten with a little stock and cook for 1 minute, then add chicken, pork and soy sauces and cook for 2 minutes. Add prawns and cook for 1 minute. Add bean sprouts and spring onion and cook for another minute or two. Serve on a large warmed platter, topped with shredded lettuce, crisp-fried shallots and lemon wedges for squeezing over the lot.

29. Chilli Prawn Noodles

Traditionally, Singapore's famous, finger-licking chilli crab and chilli prawn dishes are mopped up with slices of fresh, commercial white bread. In this dish, the luscious sweet/spicy sauce comes with its own inbuilt mopping–up agent in the form of Hokkien noodles. While not strictly authentic, it is strictly delicious.

Time: 20m

Serves: 4

Ingredients:

- 1 lb. green (raw) prawns, unpeeled
- 2 tbsp peanut oil
- 2½ cups chicken stock
- 1 clove garlic, crushed
- 2 tbsp sweet chilli sauce (e.g. Lingham's SOS brand)
- 4 tbsp tomato sauce or ketchup
- ½ tsp salt
- 1 tsp sugar
- 1 tsp corn flour - dissolve in 1 tbsp water
- 4 spring onions, chopped
- 1 egg white, beaten
- 14 oz fresh Hokkien noodles

Instructions:

Devein prawns by hooking out the black intestinal tract with a fine bamboo skewer. Heat oil in a and fry prawns for 1 to 2 minutes until they turn red. Add chicken stock and simmer for 1 minute. Add garlic, chilli sauce, tomato sauce, salt and sugar. Mix well.

Add cornflour paste, bring to boil. Stir for 60 seconds. Add half the spring onion and toss well. Slowly dribble egg white into the sauce (a good trick is to pour it through the tines of a fork), stirring constantly, until the sauce thickens.

Pour boiling water over noodles in a heatproof bowl, leave to stand for 2 minutes and drain. Arrange on a serving platter and pour prawns and sauce on top. Scatter with remaining spring onion.

30. Khanom Jeen With Spicy Pork

Yet another Oriental alternative to good old spag bol, and this time it even comes with tomato. The soft, bland nature of the rice noodles is the perfect foil for the intensely spicy sauce, proving that opposites not only attract, they can get on like a house on fire.

Time: 20m

Serves: 4

Ingredients:

- 1 tbsp vegetable oil
- 2 tbsp Thai red curry paste
- 1 tsp ground turmeric
- 1 ½ lb. minced pork
- 3 tomatoes, cut into wedges
- 1 tbsp yellow bean sauce (taucheo), mashed
- 2 tbsp fish sauce (nam pla)
- 1 tbsp lime juice
- 1 lb. Fresh round rice noodles (khanom jeen), or thin bun noodles
- 4 tbsp crisp garlic flakes (available from Asian grocery stores)
- 1 ½ cups coriander leaves
- 2 spring onions, green part only, finely sliced
- 1 ½ cups bean sprouts
- 1 lime, cut into wedges

Instructions:

Heat oil in a hot wok and fry curry paste and turmeric for 1 minute. Add minced pork and stir well. Reduce heat and gently stir fry for 4 to 5 minutes. Add tomato and cook for 3 to 4 minutes. Add bean sauce, fish sauce and lime juice. Cover and keep warm.

Pour boiling water over noodles and separate them gently with a chopstick. Drain well and arrange on a large serving platter. Pour sauce over the noodles and mix well. Scatter with garlic flakes, coriander leaves and spring onion and serve with bean sprouts and lime wedges on the side. Serve with forks and spoons.

Conclusion

And there you have it! 30 delicious noodle recipes inspired by Asian flavours to whip up in no time for the amateur home cook! Will you go with a classic and elegant soup based recipe, or perhaps a more indulgent and delicious is more to your liking? Whatever you choose, you'll end up with a delicious meal waiting to be devoured! I hope you had as much fun making these recipes as I've had coming up with them!

About the Author

A native of Indianapolis, Indiana, Valeria Ray found her passion for cooking while she was studying English Literature at Oakland City University. She decided to try a cooking course with her friends and the experience changed her forever. She enrolled at the Art Institute of Indiana which offered extensive courses in the culinary Arts. Once Ray dipped her toe in the cooking world, she never looked back.

When Valeria graduated, she worked in French restaurants in the Indianapolis area until she became the head chef at one of the 5-star establishments in the area. Valeria's attention to taste and visual detail caught the eye of a local business person who expressed an interest in publishing her recipes. Valeria began her secondary career authoring cookbooks and e-books which she tackled with as much talent and gusto as her first career. Her passion for food leaps off the page of her books which have colourful anecdotes and stunning pictures of dishes she has prepared herself.

Valeria Ray lives in Indianapolis with her husband of 15 years, Tom, her daughter, Isobel and their loveable Golden Retriever, Goldy. Valeria enjoys cooking special dishes in her large, comfortable kitchen where the family gets involved in preparing meals. This successful, dynamic chef is an inspiration to culinary students and novice cooks everywhere.

Author's Afterthoughts

Thank you for Purchasing my book and taking the time to read it from front to back. I am always grateful when a reader chooses my work and I hope you enjoyed it!

With the vast selection available online, I am touched that you chose to be purchasing my work and take valuable time out of your life to read it. My hope is that you feel you made the right decision.

I very much would like to know what you thought of the book. Please take the time to write an honest and informative review on Amazon.com. Your experience and opinions will be of great benefit to me and those readers looking to make an informed choice.

With much thanks,

Valeria Ray

Made in the USA
Middletown, DE
11 November 2022

14692937R00061